INVENTORS & INVENTIONS

PHOTOGRAPHY

INVENTORS & INVENTIONS

PHOTOGRAPHY

GINI HOLLAND

BENCHMARK BOOKS

MARSHALL CAVENDISH
NEW YORK

Benchmark Books
Marshall Cavendish Corporation
99 White Plains Road
Tarrytown, New York 10591-9001

©Marshall Cavendish Corporation, 1996

Series created by The Creative Publishing Company

Library of Congress Cataloging-in-Publication Data

Holland, Gini.
    Photography / Gini Holland.
       p.   cm. -- (Inventors & inventions)
    Includes bibliographical references (p.61) and index.
    Summary: Describes the photographic process and the development of
photography from early simple cameras through various technological
advances to modern links with computers.
    ISBN 0-7614-0066-4
    1. Photography--History--Juvenile literature.   [1. Photography-
-History.] I. Title. II. Series.
TR149.H627   1995
770'.9--dc20   95-15270
                                                 CIP
                                                 AC

Printed and bound in Hong Kong

Acknowledgments

Technical Consultant: Steven L. Barnicki, Ph.D.
Illustrations on pages 43 and 44 by Julian Baker

The publishers would like to thank the following for their permission to reproduce photographs:
The Bridgeman Art Library Ltd, (8 – By courtesy of the Board of Trustees of the V & A, 50 – By courtesy of the Fitzwilliam Museum, Cambridge); Mary Evans Picture Library, (19); The Hulton Deutsch Collection Ltd, (22); Magnum Photos, Inc, (Elliott Erwitt 39); Pedro Meyer, (56, 57); Science Photo Library Ltd, (13, 14, 24, 29, Professor Harold Edgerton frontispiece, NASA 7, Philippe Plailly 48, Roger Ressmeyer/Starlight 52); Science & Society Picture Library, (15, 16, 17, 18, 21, 23, 27, 28, 42); Robert Scott Associates, (54, 59, Trevor S. Payne 53, 58); Tony Stone Images, (front cover); UPI/Bettmann, (9, 11, 25, 26, 31, 34, 35, 36, 38, 40, 46, 47, 49); James Van Der Zee, (Van Der Zee with Violin, 1931 – Courtesy Donna Van Der Zee, 32, Couple in Raccoon Coats, 1932 – Courtesy Donna Van Der Zee, 33).

(Cover) A cheetah poses for tourists' cameras.

(Frontispiece) A series of high-speed photos of pole vaulter David Tork in action at the Boston Garden in 1964.

Contents

— Chapter 1 —
First Steps

Sarah's friends look over her shoulder as she clicks a computer control. Instantly, her parents' electronic mail service is open. They listen for the musical beeps that tell them the computer modem is making a phone call. Then a friendly voice says, "Welcome!," and they know they are on-line. Now, they can click into hundreds of areas on the Internet. They could go to the encyclopedia or the homework hotline and get started on their homework.

But Sarah knows what she wants. "Let's take a look at the pictures on MTV," she suggests. "Right," Joshua agrees. "Maybe they have a new photo of Shaquille O'Neil." Sarah clicks the logo of MTV and then lets Josh open the Sports Image Bank. "Wow! They've got it!" Sarah clicks on the word *Download*, and within minutes, they're ready to print a picture of Joshua's favorite basketball player.

For a few cents on Sarah's parents' phone bill, they have a new photograph without going to the store or even picking up the phone. The photograph came into Sarah's house over the phone line. "Now it's my turn," Sarah announces. "I'm going to download a picture of my favorite skater."

A New Way of Recording

Although we see them everywhere today, 160 years ago photographs did not exist. Now, we have family albums that record almost all the events of our lives. Books and newspapers bring full color pictures from around the world, and photos show every product we can buy on huge billboards, in magazines, and on television. With home computers hooked up to modems, photographs about any subject can be downloaded over the telephone and printed within a matter of minutes. Satellites in space, robots on volcano rims, tiny cameras swallowed by patients to detect stomach problems, microscopes so powerful they can photograph atoms, and deep-sea divers' waterproof cameras all give us pictures of places that are easier to view than visit. We take photography for granted.

However, before 1839 the only way to show how something looked was to draw a picture, paint a painting, or trace it. Humans had been on the planet for over one and one-half million years, but no one had ever found a way to quickly copy anything to show to someone else.

What Photography Is and Why It Is Needed

Photography is a way of making a permanent image on light-sensitive materials. It is the parent of modern movies and videos. People couldn't make movies until they found out how to take a picture of something and keep it over time. By the time photography was finally invented, people already knew about most of the necessary principles, materials, and chemicals, but no one knew how to put them together in the right way. In this sense, photography was an invention waiting to happen. But it was a long wait.

Before photography was invented, painted portraits were the only pictures people had of one another, and in most cases, only the rich could afford them. In those days, even if you had a

Space shuttle astronaut Michael Baker photographs Earth from space. Today, cameras can give us images of the most distant planets in our solar system and reach the most inaccessible places on Earth.

Around 1600, anyone with plenty of money could commission accurate, detailed, miniature paintings like these of their family and friends. This girl was painted by Isaac Oliver in 1590.

painting of a person or a place, you could only look at it during daylight hours or by candlelight, oil lamp, or later, gaslight.

From the time of Aristotle, many scholars knew that a traceable image of an object could be projected with light onto a flat surface. Aristotle, a Greek philosopher who lived between the years 384–322 B.C., wrote about the optic facts involved in something later known as the camera obscura. The words *camera obscura* literally mean dark chamber or dark room. It is a tracing tool used by artists beginning in the 1500s. The camera obscura works because when light reflects off an object and then travels through a small hole into a dark box, an upside-down image of that object is projected on the opposite wall of the box. Oriental and Arabic scholars at the time of Aristotle also wrote about this fact, so it was known in the ancient world, at least among those who could read. But for the next two thousand years, no one could figure out how to save that image.

Leonardo da Vinci, a famous Italian painter and scientist (1452–1519) also wrote about the camera obscura, but the Dutch astronomer Rainer Freisus was the first to use it to trace a drawing. He built a room-sized camera obscura so that he could stand inside it. Then he traced the image that came into the room onto translucent paper. He used this big camera obscura to observe the solar eclipse of 1544 and then published a drawing of the camera itself so that people could see how it was made. But although he could trace any image that the camera obscura took in, he still could not save the actual image. When the light was turned off or the sun went behind a cloud, the image disappeared.

New Tricks with Lenses and Mirrors

Then, around 1550, Gerolamo Cardano from Milan decided to place a glass lens on the hole of the camera. This made the image brighter and sharper because it could focus the light clearly onto the paper, just as the lenses in eyeglasses help people focus their eyes. With the lens in place, the camera obscura became more popular. Toward the end of the 1500s, Giambattista della Porta, an Italian, showed artists it was a useful tracing tool. Finally, in 1685, the German Johann Zahn put a mirror in the box to turn the image right side up before it hit the paper so the tracing could be made right side up in the first place.

By this time, the camera obscura ranged in size from a small closet to a simple box or booklike device that could be set on a table. It was called a camera, but it couldn't make a photograph. For that, a new discovery was needed. Someone had to find a chemical that would react to light by getting darker and then stop getting darker when the image was fully formed.

This eighteenth-century engraving explains how the camera obscura works. Light reflects off a house and shines through the hole of a camera, or box, creating an upside-down image of the house on the far wall of the camera.

The Search for Chemicals

In 1727, Germany's Johann Heinrich Schulze discovered that silver nitrate darkens when exposed to light. He demonstrated that with these silver salts, you could "write with light." He cut letters out of a piece of paper and wrapped the paper around a bottle of silver salts. He was amazed to see what happened next. Excited, he wrote that "the rays of the sun passing through the slits in the paper had written words and phrases" onto the salts in the bottle.

This chemical reaction could have been the missing piece of the photography puzzle except for one thing. There was no way to stop the reaction. When the paper was taken away, light hit *all* the salts, not just the salts that were "written on" by the sun coming through Schulze's cuts in the paper. The longer Schulze looked at the letters in the light, the darker the salt around the letters became, until the letters disappeared.

However, Schulze was onto something. Around the world, other inventors began to search for ways to use silver salts to capture images permanently on paper or some other surface.

In the early 1800s, Thomas Wedgwood and Sir Humphrey Davy used silver salts to make something they called photograms. They took the silver salts out of the bottle and put them where they wanted a picture to be, on paper. To do this, they soaked paper in silver nitrate, a colorless crystal that dissolves easily in water and turns grayish black when exposed to light in the right way. Then, they put objects on the paper and put the paper in sunlight. The area around the objects got darker, but the area underneath them stayed light, so that a silhouette of the objects remained on the paper for a while after the objects were removed.

But Wedgwood and Davy couldn't stop the process chemically any better than Schulze could. The longer they looked at their photograms, the more the objects' silhouettes faded away. So photograms were only a record of an object's shape as long as you didn't look at them long and kept them in a very dark place.

AMAZING FACTS

When photography was invented, the telegraph cable was not yet laid across the Atlantic and would not be until 1866. So when the first photograph was made in 1826, communication was still limited to talking face to face, writing letters, and drawing. Thomas Edison had not yet invented the light bulb or phonograph, which first recorded sound. Nothing was recorded with the accuracy we know today nor communicated quickly.

Chapter 2
The Fathers of Photography

After many false starts, photography was finally invented at about the same time by people who lived in different parts of the world. The first known photograph was made in 1826, when Joseph Nicéphore Niepce, a French chemist, put bitumen of Judea on a polished pewter plate. Bitumen of Judea is a tar-like substance used in printmaking. Then Niepce placed that plate in a camera obscura, leaving it there for over eight hours. When he took it out, he had made the first fuzzy photograph. The picture showed a view from his window, mostly parts of his roof. If you look at it very carefully, you may also be able to see the outline of a tree. For the first time in history, a realistic picture had been produced without anyone drawing it.

Now we have better chemicals so we can expose photographic film for much less than a second, giving us very sharp pictures. However, since Niepce's first photograph took eight hours, the rooftops that he recorded on his pewter plate were sunstruck first on one side, then in the middle, then on the other. This made the photograph look out of focus.

Nicéphore Niepce took the world's first photograph from his window in 1826. From then until his death in 1833, Niepce tried to improve the photographic process, searching for better chemicals to increase the sensitivity of the plate's coating and to fix the developing process.

Niepce had also created the first negative on paper, in 1816, while working with silver salts. A negative is an image in which the light areas that are pictured appear dark, and the dark areas appear light. For example, in a negative, a person's teeth appear to be black instead of white, while the pupils in their eyes are white instead of black. So Niepce's first attempt at making a photograph came out backwards!

He also had trouble stopping the process, just as Wedgwood and Davy had done. Perhaps that is why Niepce turned away from using chemicals on paper and started to work with other chemicals on metal instead. Niepce's picture on a pewter plate was the first known positive photograph. A positive is any photographic print or slide film that shows light and dark areas (or, in color photography, actual colors) the way they really are. In modern film photography, a negative is made on film, which is then developed so that positive prints can be made from it.

In 1827, Niepce began a partnership with artist Louis Jacques Mandé Daguerre that lasted until Niepce's death in 1833. Niepce was not happy with bitumen of Judea, because it reacted too slowly to sunlight. Daguerre had been working with silver iodide, which he made by spreading fumes of iodine over a highly polished, silver-coated copper plate. To make the plate shiny enough to show a picture, he then polished it again, giving it a mirrorlike surface. Then, he put the plate inside a camera. The camera that Daguerre used was the same type of camera obscura that Niepce had used, with a glass lens over the hole to focus light on the inside of the box. Daguerre made sure his polished plate was in position at the focal point of the lens.

Like Niepce, Daguerre had to let the light shine on the plate for a long time. Then he took the plate out and exposed it to vapors of heated mercury. Like magic, the image appeared on the plate. When the image was dark enough to be seen clearly, he stopped it from getting darker, or "fixed" it, by putting the plate in a bath of ordinary salt. The picture he made was clear and full of detail. On January 7, 1839, a member of the prestigious French Académie des Sciences and a promoter of Daguerre and Niepce, François Arago (with permission from Daguerre and Niepce's widow, Isadore Niepce) announced the invention to the Académie. Arago called it the daguerreotype, after Daguerre.

1839: A Big Year for Photography

In the same year that Daguerre and Niepce's inventions were announced, William Henry Fox Talbot, working in Britain, had made a paper negative from which unlimited paper positives could be made. He called it a calotype. It was not as sharp and clear as the daguerreotype, but his paper only had to be exposed for twenty seconds in strong light, so it was much faster than the daguerreotype. After Fox Talbot exposed his paper, he washed the paper in a bath of gallic acid and silver nitrate, and the image appeared on the paper. He had also worked out a way to fix his images so that they wouldn't disappear. It wasn't perfect yet, but it did the job.

When he heard about Daguerre's announcement, Fox Talbot got worried. He'd been working to make the first photograph, and now Daguerre was going to get all the credit for the breakthrough. So he quickly wrote both the French Académie and the English Royal Society about his work. But it was too late. Their inventions were announced within weeks of one another, but Daguerre had beaten him in the race to announce the invention of a real photograph. Fox Talbot was very bitter.

This, the oldest surviving daguerrotype, portrays Dorothy Draper in 1840. It was taken by her brother, John William Draper, who, with Samuel Morse, introduced the daguerrotype to the United States. In 1840, Draper was the first to photograph the Moon and he took the first microphotographs to illustrate a book on physiology in 1850.

William Henry Fox Talbot (1800–1877)

Fox Talbot was a mathematician and scientist who came from a wealthy aristocratic family. He lived his entire life in Lacock Abbey, his family home for generations. Parts of it were built in the 1300s, some five hundred years before he was born. Many of his first calotypes show his servants at work around this abbey and reveal his elegant lifestyle. Lacock Abbey is now a museum of his work and equipment.

Fox Talbot earned both his undergraduate and master of arts degrees at Trinity College, Cambridge, England. He loved to study and experiment and, because of his wealth, was able to travel and search for archaeological treasures. He spoke Assyrian and was one of the first men to figure out the cuneiform writings brought back to England from the ruins of Nineveh, which was the capital of the ancient Assyrian Empire in present-day Iraq. A member of the Royal Astronomical Society, he published works on astronomy and mathematics. He also briefly served in the local government.

A lifelong interest was established when Fox Talbot worked with the camera obscura while on his honeymoon in Italy and on archaeological trips. He studied the problem of saving the camera's image and started putting the ideas of other people together in new ways.

After inventing the calotype in 1839, Fox Talbot published a description of his invention in the first book ever illustrated with photographs. He called it *The Pencil of Nature* (1844–46) and included twenty-four original prints of his own paper calotypes. He then made more discoveries, including a way to take instant photographs using electric spark illumination

A daguerrotype of Fox Talbot in 1844.

Fox Talbot's book The Pencil of Nature *with some of the calotype prints it contains.*

(1851), a way to make photographic engravings (1852), and an albumen (egg white) gloss on photographic prints (1853). He patented his inventions to get credit for his ideas, but other scientists complained that his patents kept them from experimenting with and improving his methods. Eventually, Fox Talbot released information about his processes so others could experiment with them as well.

Although Daguerre got all the credit at first, it was Fox Talbot's invention of the calotype that led directly to the photography methods used in film today. Daguerre's invention was a dead end because the materials he used did not lead to better methods or multiple prints. The French finally honored Fox Talbot and his invention by awarding him the gold medal at the Paris Exhibition of 1867. His portrait is now included in the collection of "Fathers of Photography" in the Science Museum, London, England.

Photographs by Hippolyte Bayard, taken during a fire at a mill. A pioneer in photo techniques, Bayard took many photographs and held the first photo exhibition in 1839.

But the wealthy Englishman didn't mind taking ideas from other scientists to improve his own inventions. In 1819, Sir John Herschel had discovered that hypo-sulfate worked as a fixing agent for sensitized paper images. In 1839, when he heard about Daguerre's invention, Herschel decided to try to do the same thing. As he experimented, he accidently discovered the latent image, an image made on light-sensitive material that only appears when it is exposed to the right chemicals. He called his process photography, from the Greek words *photos* (light) and *graphia* (writing). Herschel also gave us the terms *negative* and *positive* for the two parts of the process. Fox Talbot quickly learned about Herschel's work and used Herschel's method to wash away the silver salts and stop his own calotypes, which he later called Talbotypes, from fading over time.

Another inventor, a French bureaucrat named Hippolyte Bayard, had also been hard at work in 1839. He invented a way to make photos with silver chloride. When silver chloride is exposed to light, it changes color and becomes a grayish blue. This response to light is what makes most photographic processes work. Bayard dipped his paper in potassium iodide and exposed it in the camera to yield a positive paper print. In June of 1839, Bayard had enough photographs to put together the world's first photo exhibit. He showed thirty prints and was on his way to making history, if not a lot of money. Unfortunately, he got poor advice about the patent process.

Secret Plots, French Gifts, and Progress

Daguerre, Fox Talbot, Bayard, and others began to fight for credit for this wonderful invention. Each one wanted to be known as the inventor of photography. Perhaps more important-ly, they each wanted the patent so that they could make money. The person who owned the patent could either sell it or get paid each time the invention was used.

On June 30, 1839, France bought the patent for the daguerreotype from Daguerre and gave it to the world; anyone in the world could use the invention for free. The French government paid pensions for life to Daguerre, who got six thousand francs a year, and to Niepce's son, who received four thousand francs a year.

In the original daguerrotype camera, a glass lens was placed over the hole to focus light onto a polished plate on the opposite side of the box. The plate was then removed and exposed to heated mercury vapor, which made the image appear on the plate.

However, before Daguerre sold his patent to the French government, he had secretly patented his and Niepce's invention in Britain. As a result, the daguerreotype spread quickly everywhere but Britain because the patent there made it more expensive.

While he was working with the French government to sell Daguerre's patent, Arago lied to Bayard. He told Bayard that his research needed more work and gave him six hundred francs to buy a new camera. Trusting Arago, who was his main access to the French Académie des Sciences, Bayard kept working on his research, taking more and more pictures.

By the time Bayard realized he had been tricked, it was too late. Arago had helped Daguerre and Niepce get their invention patented before Bayard could and sold it to the French government. By getting the first patent, Daguerre and Niepce also got credit for being the inventors of photography.

A hand-colored daguerrotype from the 1850s. Portrait photography quickly gained popularity among the middle class. Although the subjects had to pose motionless for a long time for a daguerrotype, it took less time than sitting for a painting and was a lot cheaper.

Bayard was angry and wanted the public to know that he had been unfairly treated. So he staged his own death and photographed himself. Next to the picture, he wrote, "The body you see is that of M. Bayard, inventor of the process with which you are now familiar. . . . The government, which gave M. Daguerre too much, said it could do nothing for Bayard at all, and the wretch drowned himself." This was one of the first, if not *the* first, photographic hoax. It was clear, even to the inventors of photography, that their invention could be used to fool people in ways that paintings never could.

Watching what was happening in France from his home in England, Fox Talbot patented his calotype process. He could not claim to be the first to give photography to the world, but his invention would now be safe. It was a different way to make photographs than the metal daguerreotype. Once patented, no one would be allowed to use it without paying him first.

Drawbacks to the Daguerreotype and Calotype

Although the daguerreotype and calotype were wonderful breakthroughs in the world of pictures, they still had problems. The chemically treated metal of the daguerreotype had to be exposed to light for a long time so people had to sit very still for longer than was comfortable or natural. Their faces looked stiff and wooden. Some photographers made uncomfortable props that held a person's head still from behind.

Unlike the paper negative of the calotype, the daguerreotype was very clear, but it was a positive print. It lacked a negative from which other copies could be made, and since it was formed on metal, light could not be shined through the positive to make another print that way either. A one-of-a-kind photograph, it was also very easily scratched and usually kept in a velvet-lined case. Its metal surface was so shiny that it gave off an annoying glare, and the picture could only be seen clearly when light hit it from just the right angle. On the other hand, the calotype's paper negative could make many prints, but the pictures were fuzzy and lacked the details that were so clear in the daguerreotype.

Photography Quickly Becomes Popular

Photography caught on fast because the people of this time, called the Victorians because Queen Victoria was on the throne of Britain, loved anything new. Not stuck in their ways, the Victorians were eager for anything that promised to amuse them.

But photography wasn't only amusing; it served a real need. Photography made portraits available to the middle class, who could not afford painted family portraits. Not only was it cheaper, but photography was lifelike. A painter could sometimes make a person look much nicer in a portrait than he or she appeared in real life. But with photography, the Victorians were now able to take inexpensive photographs that honestly showed how a person looked at the time. In spite of Bayard's hoax, most people believed that "the camera doesn't lie." At that time, and certainly compared to many paintings, this was generally true. For the first time in history, people could record themselves, their families, friends, and the world around them with true-to-life accuracy.

> **AMAZING FACTS**
>
> Félix Nadar went up in a balloon and took the first aerial photographs. He then began to use aerial photos to make maps and survey the land. In addition, he invented the photo-essay; with a series of pictures and a short written commentary, photography could tell a story.

Félix Nadar used the inventions of others to make advances in photography. He opened a photographic studio in Paris in 1853 and took portraits of the famous people who gathered there.

— Chapter 3 —
A Revolution in Film

There were two main changes in photography from 1839 to 1850. Better chemicals were found so that the process was easier, and sharper lenses were made, so that exposure times could be shorter, sometimes just a few seconds. The faster the photographer took the picture, the easier it was to catch subjects in natural poses and activities. Photography was beginning to show the world as it really was.

It was not the son of Niepce, but his nephew Claude Félix Abel Niepce de Saint-Victor who found the next chemical process for photography. Like his uncle, Niepce de Saint-Victor was also a chemist. In 1847, he invented the albumen-on-glass process. Albumen, or simple egg white, is something most cooks use everyday. Niepce de Saint Victor combined it with potassium iodide and silver acetonitrate and spread it evenly on a glass plate. He then exposed the plate for between five and fifteen minutes to get a photograph.

Two years later, in 1849, another Frenchman named Le Gray dissolved powdered cotton in ether to make a collodion base, which is a mixture in which one substance is divided into tiny particles and spread evenly throughout the second substance. He used this collodion base to make his negative sensitive to light. Then, in 1851 the Englishman Frederick Scott Archer published a version of this wet collodion process, having found an emulsion, or coating, of silver iodide that would stick to glass. He exposed the glass plate while it was still wet with the emulsion and then developed this negative immediately by "fixing" it, or stopping the chemical process, and then drying it. Then Archer shone a light through the negative on the glass to make a positive photo. The finished picture was as full of detail as a daguerreotype but could be printed again and again, like a calotype. This soon became popularly known as the "wet plate" process.

This process took more skill than a daguerreotype or calotype did, and it had to be developed right away. But photographers could take it outside, often traveling in photography wagons fixed up with the chemicals and the dark space they needed. Sometimes traveling photographers would use light-proof tents instead.

The wet plate process advanced photography both as a science and as an art. Landscapes could be photographed in sharp detail, and visual reports could be made from battlefields.

Unfortunately for Archer, while he published a description of his wet plate process, he failed to patent it. Without the patent rights, he could not make any money off of his and Le Gray's invention so he died penniless.

AMAZING FACTS

In order to take bigger pictures, Thomas Sutton replaced the glass lens with a water-filled sphere in 1859, inventing the first wide-angle lens. It became known as the panoramic liquid lens because it took a wide enough picture to shoot an entire panorama, or landscape.

The wet plate process required a lot of equipment to develop plates immediately. So photographers carried several chemicals and a dark room with them as well as the camera itself.

Julia Margaret Cameron (1815–1879)

Julia Margaret Cameron was a pioneer photographer when photography was new. People in her day usually did not believe in women doing anything outside of the home, and Cameron accepted her roles of wife and mother. However, with patience and hard work, she also became a professional photographer.

Cameron's family was in the highest ranks of the British civil service, and she was born in Calcutta, India, where they were posted. During her youth, she lived with her grandmother in France and was educated in Europe. Then she married a member of the British civil service and returned to India, where she lived for ten years. When her husband retired, they moved to England.

Cameron was given her first camera by her daughter and son-in-law when she was forty-eight years old. She then built her own

photography studio and mastered the wet plate (collodion) process. One year later, in 1864, she was making prints and giving albums of them to her friends. The same year, she was elected a member of the photographic societies of London and Scotland. She began to show her work and sell it professionally.

Because of her high place in society and her interest in the arts, Cameron had many important friends, including Alfred, Lord Tennyson, the poet, and his wife. She took photographs of them as well as of the American poet Henry Wadsworth Longfellow, the photographic inventor Sir John Herschel, and many others. In this way, she gave future generations a wonderful record of some of the most famous people of her time. Known for her dramatic portraits and for photographs that illustrate poems and religious scenes, she worked with Tennyson to illustrate his *Idylls of the King*, published in 1875.

Cameron's portrait of the poet, Alfred, Lord Tennyson.

Cameron worked to make photography accepted as an art. Her portraits were different from the stiff, formal pictures taken by most other photographers in her day. Many of her portraits look natural, as if she caught the person unaware. In fact, she usually had to make her subjects sit for a long exposure time. Many of her pictures were criticized because she used a soft focus, took close-up shots, and experimented with lighting. Her work is enjoyed today because it shows the character and spirit of the people she photographed.

Then, in 1871 the English doctor Richard Leach Maddox developed dry plate photography. His glass plates were treated with a gelatin and silver-salt coating that made the plates light-sensitive even though they were dry. This really freed photographers. They didn't have to prepare a wet plate in a dark room or light-proof tent. They didn't need to rush it to a waiting camera in a light-proof holder, take the photo, and bring it back to the darkroom while it was still wet. With Maddox's dry plate, photographers put the plate in the camera, exposed it when they were ready, and developed it later.

British-American photographer Eadweard Muybridge (1830–1904) put a series of cameras along a racetrack to prove that a trotting horse at one point actually has all four legs in the air. In 1878, he wrote The Horse In Motion, *illustrated with his photographs, allowing artists to make accurate paintings of a running horse for the first time.*

George Eastman Changes Everything

George Eastman was an American bank teller who was caught up in the photography craze along with so many others of his generation. Frustrated by the wet plate process, in which the plate had to be developed right away before it dried, he, too, experimented to find a way to make a dry plate that could be developed whenever the photographer wanted. He finally succeeded and opened his Dry Plate Company in 1881. Then he and William H. Walker invented a container for rolls of negative paper in 1884.

Taking this roll idea further, in 1885 the two men made a kind of thin film they called Eastman America. After this film was exposed in the camera, it could be rolled into the container with the help of a paper backing. When the film was developed in the darkroom, the paper backing was thrown away. To complete the process and make a photograph, Eastman then put the thin negative film onto glass, placed light-sensitive paper under

AMAZING FACTS

In 1880, Eadweard Muybridge invented the zoopraxiscope, which projected light through a series of still pictures on a spinning glass plate. The images looked as though they were moving — thus, the first motion picture.

it, shone light through the negative onto the paper, and made a positive print.

Then, in 1888 came the invention that made photography truly accessible to everyone — the Kodak. Eastman's Kodak was one of the first cameras to use roll film. In 1889, he began to market his camera preloaded with this film. His slogan was "You press the button, we'll do the rest." The loaded Kodak had enough film for one hundred pictures, and the directions were simple enough for a child to use.

The camera was small enough to hold in one hand, and best of all, Kodak did the developing for the photographer. Unlike

A woman using a Kodak box camera around 1890. The Kodak was the first camera to be mass-produced cheaply. This, and the fact it was simple to use, made it immediately popular.

the wet collodion process, with the Kodak system the amateur was freed from working in the darkroom with chemicals and paper. Instead, Eastman had his customers send him the entire camera for film development. Then he returned the original camera, reloaded with fresh film and ready to go, along with the pictures he had developed for them.

George Eastman wanted to market his product in a big way from the start. He made up the word *Kodak* so that his camera would have a name that was simple enough to be said easily and remembered in any country. He also made it affordable for the middle class. Eastman's low cost and easy method revolutionized photography and helped make it available to everyone.

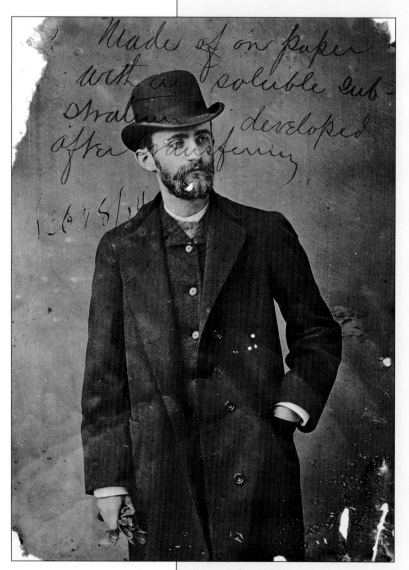

George Eastman in 1884. This is a test photo covered with Eastman's own notes.

George Eastman (1854–1932)

George Eastman was born in Waterville, New York. His early years were not easy. His father had put the family's money into a business school that failed when students went off to fight in the Civil War, and one of Eastman's three sisters was crippled by polio. Then his father died when Eastman was just seven years old, and Eastman's mother had to rent rooms to boarders to bring in money. To help out, at age thirteen Eastman got his first job, as a messenger boy for three dollars a week. He worked and studied hard and always recorded his expenses and income. His care with money helped him get a job as a junior bookkeeper at the Rochester Savings Bank when he was twenty years old. He was finally able to not only support his mother but put some money in savings as well. He could even afford to start dabbling in photography.

Although just a hobby at first, the wet plates, camera, and chemicals of photography were so much work that Eastman decided to invent an easier way. He worked in the bank all day and spent his nights stirring chemicals in his mother's kitchen. Finally, he made a dry plate gelatin emulsion, a coating for the photographic plate that did not have to stay wet to be used. Then, he invented a machine to make the new kind of plates, rented some factory space, and began his Dry Plate Company in 1881. This was one of the first companies in America to mass-produce a product. In ten months, his factory was selling four thousand plates a month.

However, his customers soon started sending the plates back because they clouded over with a red fog before photographers could use them. In what was one of the first instances of "factory recall" in the history of industrialization, Eastman recalled all the plates he had sold and worked incessantly to find the problem. He didn't even go home at night, instead sleeping in a hammock in his factory. Finally, Eastman realized that it was the gelatin he was using that was at fault. He ordered some better gelatin and decided to always test his materials before he used them.

Wanting to make photography easier, Eastman invented roll film in 1888. Since most photographers stayed with their old plate cameras, Eastman invented the Kodak camera as a way to sell his film. The plan worked. The Kodak was easy to use, and his company mass-produced it cheaply, helping make photography a popular hobby. Eastman's factory had a profit-sharing plan for his workers, and in his lifetime, he gave over $100 million to universities in the United States and Europe. His company continues to research new products and remains a world leader in films, photographic papers, and cameras.

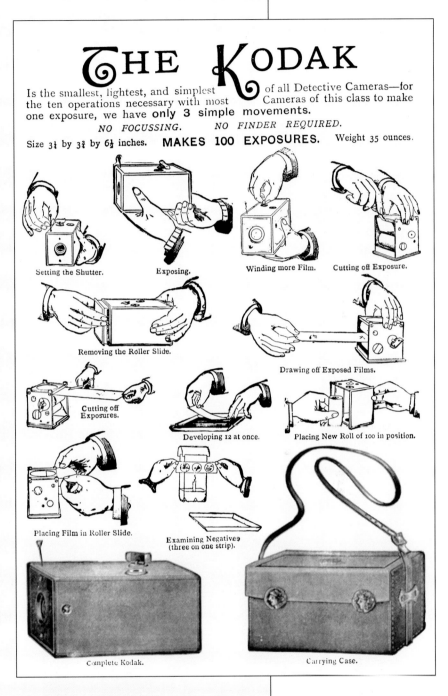

An 1889 advertisement shows the public how easy it is to use a Kodak camera.

Cameras of All Sizes

The bicycle craze begun in the mid-1880s and continuing through the 1890s had started a trend toward photography on wheels even without the Kodak. Before the Kodak caught on with the public, many photographers could be seen lugging bulky tripods and photo equipment out into the streets and countryside on the seats of their tall, old-fashioned bicycles.

Fortunately, cameras kept getting simpler and cheaper. In 1894, the tiny Kombi camera, so-called because it combined the ability to take pictures (from positive film, like slides) with a viewer for looking at them, sold for about $3.00. Its viewer magnified the pictures about three times. Film for 125 pictures was available for $1.00, and a film developing kit sold for $3.00.

At about the same time, the largest camera ever made was invented in order to take a single negative of a very wide picture. It was commissioned by the Chicago & Alton Railroad to make a "perfect portrait" of its new luxury train. The owners of the railroad wanted a single negative to capture the entire train. They didn't want two or three negatives put together, which would be the only other way to show the entire train in complete detail. So they hired George R. Lawrence to make a camera that could take a photo no less than eight feet long. The biggest camera ever made, the Mammoth weighed seven tons and needed fifteen men to work it. Ten gallons of chemicals were needed to make the one 4.5-by-8-foot print of the train. In 1900, a photo taken by the Mammoth won the Grand Prize of the World at the Paris Exposition.

The Mammoth camera, the largest ever, is erected in Chicago in 1900. Its usefulness was limited, however, and the general trend was toward smaller, lightweight cameras.

Photos in Print

Along with Eastman's roll film revolution, another important change helped make photographs affordable and easy to print in newspapers and magazines. The development of the half-tone plate in the closing years of the nineteenth century made printing photos in newspapers, books, and magazines economically possible for the first time. This gave rise to news photography and photojournalism. Before the half-tone plate was invented, no shades of gray could be printed in newspapers. A photograph that does not have shades of gray is only black and white and cannot show any detail or three-dimensional shapes as it only shows the silhouette of an object. Printing presses used only black ink on white paper so they weren't set up to show photographs. Drawings could use cross-hatching to shade areas and give a picture detail, but photographs printed in newspapers lost all their detail and shades of gray. To solve the problem, gray tones had to be shown in a new way.

The key was to use a screen of fine lines on glass that broke the photographic image into thousands of dots. This dot pattern was then transferred photographically onto a chemically treated printing plate that then printed all the tones. For the first time, photos could be printed on the same press with type. Since this change happened at the same time as the invention of dry plates, flexible film, and hand-held cameras, photography at the turn of the century quickly became easier and more widely used than ever before.

This is one of the first underwater photos, shot by French zoologist Louis Boutan in 1893. It was made possible by using a magnesium flash.

— Chapter 4 —
Cameras Hide, Seek, and Tell All

At the turn of the century, cameras were seen by many as middle-class toys. Wanting to look rich and upper class, many wealthy Europeans, Asians, and Americans did not want to be seen carrying them. But many of them also wanted to play with this engaging new toy. This led to some clever camera disguises, including the binocular cameras in use in the 1860s through the 1880s. There were also at least twelve kinds of "book" cameras disguised for the same reason. Since many of the rich were proud to be seen using binoculars and books but embarrassed to be seen using cameras, these hidden cameras were widely sold.

However, they were usually hard to use, and some of the binocular cameras actually had to be used backwards. The "secret" photographer who used these had to look through the large end of the binoculars and point the smaller end toward whatever the person wanted to photograph. So a person who didn't want to look middle class by using a camera probably looked rather silly looking through the wrong end of binoculars.

Other Odd Steps Toward Secrecy

Detectives were another group of people who wanted to keep their picture taking a secret. Camera makers created special devices for them, such as the hat camera of 1891, which guaranteed good photos — and a perfect fit for the photographer's head! Another secret device was the vest camera, first sold in 1886.

Advertised as "of great value to artists and detectives," the vest camera took four or five circular pictures on a plate. Lacking a viewfinder, the operator simply pointed the vest on his chest toward the subject and hoped for the best. However, if the photographer with a vest camera was very fat, he usually just took photos of the sky.

The tie pin camera of the 1890s also promised to be invisible and secretive but had the same drawbacks as the vest camera. It's hard to get a good photo from any camera when you can't look through a viewfinder to see what you're framing for the film.

A woman shooting flowers around a pond. Photography had become a popular middle-class hobby by 1905 when this picture was taken.

Since many cities had three or more privately run newspapers in the 1920s and 1930s, newspapers competed hard for scoops and photo firsts. A good photograph could sell a lot of newspapers, especially if no one else could get the picture. This situation promoted the development and use of more secret camera devices, including the woman's powder-box camera of the 1920s. Since many women in those days carried a powder compact with them, this was seen as a good disguise for a woman reporter's camera. No one would think that a woman was taking a picture when she held the compact mirror up to her eyes; they would think she was just checking her makeup. Since she could hold it in a way that allowed her to look through the viewfinder, this worked better than the vest and tie pin cameras.

Unusual newspaper stories needed unusual cameras, especially when photographers were not allowed in the building, such as in courtrooms and jails. The execution camera, made to be strapped around a photographer's ankle and then triggered by a long cable release, promised to help the reporter take a picture of a prisoner being executed.

James Van Der Zee (1886–1983)

James Van Der Zee lived for almost one hundred years. He photographed formal portraits, often with a story to tell, and street scenes of daily life. His work shows the lives and changes in Harlem and its African-American residents from 1915 through 1983.

James Van Der Zee in 1931.

Van Der Zee was born in the small town of Lenox, Massachusetts, in 1886. His parents, who were maid and butler for a short time to President Ulysses S. Grant, were small landowners who also ran several family businesses. In Lenox, Van Der Zee led a sheltered life, but when he opened his first photography studio in New York City in 1915, he quickly became the most popular photographer for leaders of the African-American community in Harlem. He composed his photographs well and used his artistic skills to touch up both negatives and prints so his portraits showed people at their best. He was also creative with darkroom techniques.

A musician who played both the violin and piano, Van Der Zee was an artist who needed a partner to help him with the business side of his work. He found this first in his sister Jenny, who invited him to join her at her Toussaint Conservatory of Art and Music in Harlem. But his first wife, Kate L. Brown, did not like photography because it could not provide a steady income. When their marriage broke up, Van Der Zee found both a wife and partner in Gaynella Greenlee. She was his business manager and even took some photos of her own.

He was as good as the leading photographers of the time, but Van Der Zee was not well known outside of the African-American community until the Museum of Modern Art "discovered" him in 1967. At that time, he was in deep financial trouble. After World War II, many middle-class blacks began to move out of Harlem, taking their business with them. This left Van Der Zee with fewer customers and less money. Van Der Zee and his wife were evicted from their home while he waited for money from the museum. Finally, in 1969, the museum paid him over $3,000 to exhibit enlargements of some of his forty thousand prints and negatives in a show called "Harlem on My Mind." Van Der Zee was eighty-three years old.

Couple in Raccoon Coats, *1932, by Van Der Zee.*

At age ninety-two, he married Donna Mussenden, a New York gallery director who helped the last four years of his life to be happy and productive. In 1980, comedian Bill Cosby sat for Van Der Zee's camera, and many famous people followed, sitting in the old-fashioned chairs Van Der Zee had used throughout his career.

Always a dedicated artist, James Van Der Zee said of his photos that "sometimes they seemed to be more valuable to me than they did to the people I was photographing because I put my heart and soul into them."

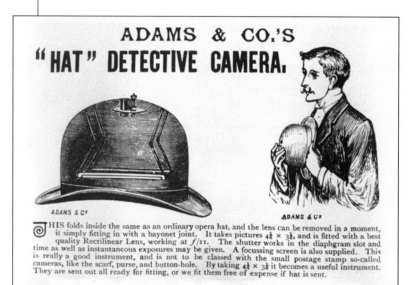

ADAMS & CO.'S "HAT" DETECTIVE CAMERA.

ADAMS & Cº

ADAMS & Cº

THIS folds inside the same as an ordinary opera hat, and the lens can be removed in a moment, it simply fitting in with a bayonet joint. It takes pictures 4¼ × 3¼, and is fitted with a best quality Rectilinear Lens, working at *f*/11. The shutter works in the diaphgram slot and time as well as instantaneous exposures may be given. A focussing screen is also supplied. This is really a good instrument, and is not to be classed with the small postage stamp so-called cameras, like the scarf, purse, and button-hole. By taking 4¼ × 3¼ it becomes a useful instrument. They are sent out all ready for fitting, or we fit them free of expense if hat is sent.

The hat camera was one of many strange devices invented to take secret pictures. They were popular with detectives involved in discreet investigations and with news photographers fighting to be the first to an interesting story.

Another example of an attempt to use an invisible camera to sell more newspapers in the old days was the not-so-invisible Talbot's Invisible Camera, which was strapped to the chest of a *Daily Mirror* photographer. Unfortunately, it was discovered before he could use it. The only news scoop that *Daily Mirror* reporter got was the news of his own arrest.

Similarly, the shoe camera was another device sold to reporters and detectives so they could take secret pictures. To snap the picture, the reporter had to press on the back of his heel. But probably not many reporters were able to take pictures with these cameras without getting caught. Since they would have to quickly press on the back of the heel and then bring one foot up in the air to frame a good picture, it would look as though they were doing a very strange dance.

Spies Disguise and Miniaturize

To solve this problem of secrecy, by the 1950s some very small cameras were developed for spies so that they could look through their camera quickly and then put it in a pocket as soon as they were finished. Some were disguised as cigarette lighters and other small objects that would look normal when not in use. The main problem for small cameras that used smaller film was that their pictures were often grainy looking and just not very sharp. During World War II, German spies got around this problem by taking pictures of important papers and then shrinking them to very small negatives afterwards. Some of the negatives they made were no bigger than the period at the end of this sentence. The spies hid the tiny negatives by putting them under the periods in their letters to Germany. Luckily, a wartime censor noticed the trick.

Other World War II spies used a camera called the Minox, which used film that showed good detail. Because it took very good photographs but was also small enough to fit easily into a pocket, it was popular with the general public after the war.

Then, in 1972 Kodacolor II film was introduced, along with a Kodak Pocket Instamatic Camera. The film was sixteen millimeter, less than half the size of the usual thirty-five-millimeter film. Fairly good prints could be made from the tiny negatives, including five-by-seven-inch and eight-by-ten-inch prints. Not just for spies, the Kodak Pocket Instamatic became popular with the general public because it was easy to carry and simple to use.

Magazines Give Photography a Boost

Before 1936, people could read about themselves and occasionally see a photograph of some social event or dramatic moment in print. But newspapers still needed artists as much as photographers to illustrate their stories because their short deadlines made it hard for daily newspapers to wait for photographs to be developed. Then *Life* magazine published its first issue. The opening photo was a full-page photograph of a doctor holding a newborn baby by the ankles, with the caption "Life begins." Its first

Press photographers wear masks at a war gas demonstration given by student officers of the Army, Navy, and Marine Corps at Edgewood, Missouri. During the 1930s, the number of professional photographers increased as new photo magazines were published.

printing, in 1936, was for 466,000 copies. Circulation reached one million in the first year and reached eight million subscriptions by 1972, its best and final year. It's estimated that with that many subscriptions going out to people's homes in 1972, about forty million people were reading the magazine and looking at its pictures.

In a big boost for photographers, *Life* magazine provided a weekly outlet and a huge audience for documentary photography. Picture magazines with national circulation gave society a mirror of itself and the world. They showed Americans to one another on a weekly basis; readers saw their fellow citizens as they were, from all parts of the country and from all walks of life. *Life* raised social issues and promoted art and science. The magazine was educational, but it also pushed trends and patriotism and promoted the conservative political and cultural values of its owner, Henry R. Luce. When he started *Life*, Luce wrote that its purpose was "To see life, to see the world, to eyewitness great events; to watch the faces of the poor and the gestures of the proud; to see strange things . . . to see and take pleasure in seeing; to see and be amazed; to see and be instructed."

The following year, *Look* magazine was first published. *Look* competed with *Life* and gave photographers another national magazine that would buy their photos.

The Great Depression and other large-scale disasters gave rise to documentary photographic essays, such as the ones by Dorothea Lange, funded by the Farm Security Administration. By taking a series of photographs about a special idea, theme, or group of people, the documentary photographer could make a statement and educate. Photographers

Dorothea Lange took this picture of a migrant agricultural worker's family in California in 1936. During the Depression in the 1930s, she made photographic records of the hardships ordinary people faced.

also developed photo stories, or a series of pictures that showed events with a beginning, middle, and end.

Life magazine continued to be popular until the moment of its death in December 1972. By this time, too many of its advertisers had left for television, where they could reach larger audiences. Without advertisers paying for space, the price of the magazine would be much too high for the average reader. *Life* published its last weekly issue on December 28, 1972. Still photos were being replaced by video images, and photographers had to find other places to sell their work. Although *Life* occasionally publishes special editions, this great outlet for photography is basically a thing of the past.

Photography Careers Past and Present

However, even as the great photo magazines passed away, photography began to be used more in daily newspapers, putting artists out of work while it gave photographers more jobs. Then, in the 1990s, some weekly magazines such as the *New Yorker*, which was founded in 1925, finally started using some photography along with their traditional drawings.

Throughout its history, photography has been a means of self-employment for many people. Often begun as a hobby, people from all walks of life have found that they can work out of their home rather than in a rented space so that the start-up costs for their business are relatively low. A camera, film, paper, chemicals, and a light-proof room in which to develop film and make prints are all you need to get started.

World War I (1914–1918) increased the demand for photographers, especially the white male photographers who were paid to cover the war. The government at that time did not hire women or minorities. However, racial segregation in the South actually helped African-American photographers start their own businesses because blacks usually had to get their pictures taken by people in their own communities.

AMAZING FACTS
In 1883, a *New York Times* article called "Photographed While Kissing" reported how photography was supposedly starting to be used to blackmail people. The article said a young woman asked a young priest to visit her home and told him she loved him. She asked for one kiss "to console her passion." He gave her a kiss, and a photo was secretly taken, with which she attempted to blackmail him. She sent him a copy of the photo and told him he could purchase the other eleven copies at twenty dollars apiece.

Dorothea Lange (1895–1965)

Dorothea Lange was a photographer of great courage and skill. Born and raised in Hoboken, New Jersey, she studied photography on her own at first and then with Clarence H. White at Columbia University. She began her career by making a darkroom out of a chicken coop.

Unhappy living with her mother, Lange left home in 1918. She and a friend had $140 between them, but they planned to work their way "around the world. " All Lange had at that time was a camera around her neck and a strong belief that she could make her living with photography. She and her friend ended up in San Francisco, where she photographed people in the streets during the Depression. Her most famous picture from this time is *White Angel Breadline* (1933).

Crippled by polio as a child, Lange had a limp for the rest of her life, making her feel different from others. Her disability taught her to care deeply about other people's pain and to understand

These unemployed workers in New Jersey were photographed by Dorothea Lange in 1936.

how terrible it feels to be unaccepted. In the 1930s, she demonstrated this sensitivity when she worked with her future husband, Paul Taylor, an economics professor, on a report about migrant workers. Her photos of the workers showed their pride and strength in spite of terrible living conditions. The report convinced the state of California to improve the camps that migrant workers lived in.

Throughout her career, Lange's photographs moved people to make changes for the better. From 1935 to 1942, her photos of American farming life, which she took for the Farm Security Administration, were published in thousands of magazines and newspapers. They showed the desperate time American farmers faced during the Depression. Simple and clear, her photos also helped change the direction of American photography toward a more realistic approach. Lange explained, "The camera is an instrument that teaches people how to see. . . ."

When Japanese-Americans were put in American internment camps during World War II, Lange was there to photograph their pain. But in 1945, she collapsed from overwork while covering a United Nations conference in San Francisco and did not work again until 1951. Then she traveled and made photo-essays for *Life* magazine. She showed many kinds of life, from *Three Mormon Towns* (1954) to *The Irish Country People* (1955). Books of her work include *An American Exodus* (with Paul Taylor, 1939) and *The American Country Woman* (1966).

Dorothea Lange in the 1960s.

A group of camera enthusiasts pose before taking a special camera train from New York to Connecticut in 1937. These pleasure trains offered developing and printing facilities to their customers.

By 1930, the U.S. Census Bureau listed 23,836 white male photographers, 7,427 white female photographers, and 547 black photographers, 85 of whom were women. From 1900 to 1930, the total number of black photographers grew 120 percent. The Great Depression of the 1930s encouraged many to take on photography as a way to make money when no one was hiring.

Today, as many people find working at home a good alternative to commuting to work, photography continues to give people a way to make an independent living. For those with personal computers, the new technologies of digital cameras, computer scanners, and software programs allow many creative uses of photographic images. The amateur working at home may continue to surprise the field of photography with homegrown innovations.

Chapter 5
New Technology Brings Greater Freedom

In the 1920s, faster black and white film helped photographers work in low light without a flash. Faster film, needing only a short exposure to light, let them shoot scenes that looked more natural and also take pictures of things that moved quickly.

Then, in 1925, the 35 mm camera was marketed for the first time. Fairly small and portable, the Leica, or candid camera, had been developed by Oskar Barnack at the Ernst Leitz company in Germany. It was the first camera to use 35 mm motion picture film, which gave better quality than Kodak film and permitted clearer enlargements. With the Leica, professional photographers freed themselves from the bulky cameras that used plates. Until then, only large cameras made good prints. Now, photographers were able to carry the small Leica everywhere and catch people in more natural poses and activities.

As with many new inventions, the Leica was not accepted right away, at least not at the big newsrooms and magazines. One member of the first team of *Life* photographers told about how tricky it was to get his Leica prints accepted by the magazine: "I had brought a Leica back from a European trip. The editor-in-chief, thinking it a toy not to be taken seriously because of its small size, forbade me to use it. At an official reception in Washington, I defied him and took a whole series of photographs in front of my . . . colleagues with their large cameras and flashes. Comparing my prints with theirs, the management admitted that my photographs were much more . . . lively

The 1925 Leica was the first 35 mm camera. The superior quality of this film made the camera popular with professional photographers, who until then had been hampered by having to carry much bulkier cameras around.

because, without the flash, I had caught the guests unaware. From then on, the Leica was appreciated; and all the photographers followed my example."

The invention of the Leica was exciting for amateur photographers as well as for professionals. Since the 35 mm camera was fairly easy to use, amateurs who were willing to learn a little about aperture (the adjustable opening that lets light into a camera) and film speed could produce better quality photographs than they could with the simple point-and-shoot Kodak cameras.

Photography Becomes Colorful

In spite of the invention of the Leica, the Kodak company was not going to fade away. There was still a big market for their simple, easy-to-use cameras. More importantly, the Kodak cameras made enough money to pay for research on new kinds of film. This led to some big breakthroughs in the 1930s. In Hungary in 1930, Bela Gaspar invented Gasparcolor, or Cibachrome, which was purchased and improved by the Eastman Kodak company, becoming Eastmancolor. This film uses a dye-destruction (or dye-bleach) method in which all the colors are present in the film and the ones not needed to make the color picture are removed by bleaching during the development stage. That same year, Leopold Mannes and Leopold Godowsky, working with Eastman Kodak Company's research staff, developed the Kodachrome method of color photography. Their method is based on the dye-coupling development process invented by Rudolf Fischer of Berlin in 1912. In this process, the dyes are injected during the development phase. In

1935, color film was made available for 16 mm motion picture cameras, and in 1937, Kodachrome color film for still camera slides was introduced. However, color negative film, which made printed pictures, was not available until 1942.

Most negative films for color photographs used a dye-incorporation method in which the chemicals that will create the dyes are set in each layer of the emulsion and are activated when the film is processed. Since these methods rely on special processing, color film could not be developed easily in the average hobbyist's home darkroom. To solve the problem, first Ansco's Ansco-color and then Kodak's Ektachrome film were brought out in 1942. But color photography was still quite expensive for the average consumer. This problem was solved in 1949, when Kodak introduced Kodacolor, from which good color prints

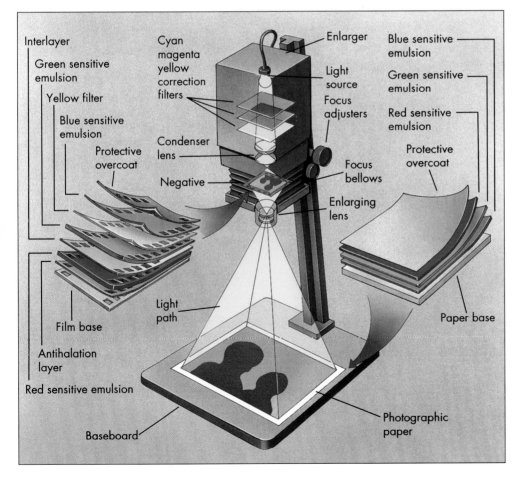

Color negative film and the paper the photograph is printed on both contain layers of emulsion that are sensitive to different colors. The light that shines through the negative and creates an image on the paper passes through colored filters.

Interlayer

Green sensitive emulsion

Yellow filter

Blue sensitive emulsion

Protective overcoat

Condenser lens

Negative

Cyan magenta yellow correction filters

Enlarger

Light source

Focus adjusters

Focus bellows

Enlarging lens

Blue sensitive emulsion

Green sensitive emulsion

Red sensitive emulsion

Protective overcoat

Light path

Film base

Antihalation layer

Red sensitive emulsion

Baseboard

Photographic paper

Paper base

could be made inexpensively. Now more affordable, color photography became increasingly popular in the fifties.

What You See Is What You Get

In 1936, the KineExacta camera, the first single-lens reflex camera, was invented in Dresden, Germany. Before this, a photographer had to look through one lens that would show something close to, but not exactly, what was framed in the camera's other, light-admitting lens. The actual picture was slightly different. This led to things like "photographic haircuts," where the photo shows part of a person's head lopped off because the photographer didn't adjust for the difference between what was seen and

Here, the basic mechanism of a single-lens reflex camera can be seen. The viewfinder allows the photographer to see exactly what will be exposed on the film. The aperture can be adjusted to let variable amounts of light into the camera, and the focal length can also be altered. When you take a picture, the mirror flips up and the shutter opens to allow light onto the film.

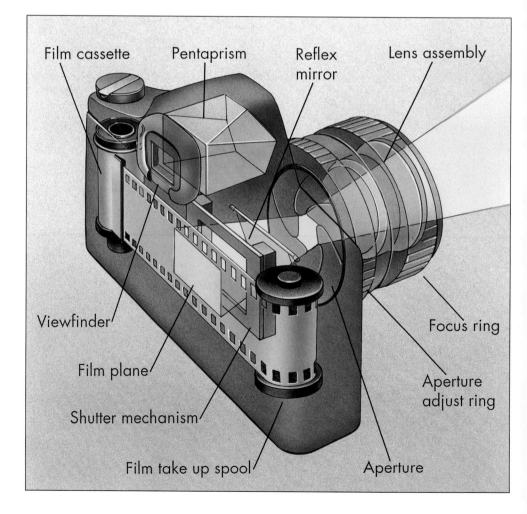

Film cassette Pentaprism Reflex mirror Lens assembly

Viewfinder

Film plane

Shutter mechanism

Film take up spool

Focus ring

Aperture adjust ring

Aperture

the real frame of the photo. Now, with the single-lens reflex camera the photographer saw exactly what the picture would look like. The camera's mirror was directly behind the shutter and flipped out of the way when the shutter was tripped. This also improved the speed with which photographers could frame the picture so they could take more natural shots.

Further Advances in Camera Technology

Countries fighting in World War II used photography as a tool and paid for photographic research as an investment in their victory. Photography was used for stress analysis to make sure metals were strong enough for planes, ships, and other fighting equipment. Aerial surveillance helped armies know where enemies were camped and where their ammunition was stored. As photographers covered war stories for their newspapers and magazines, portable lighting equipment was improved so they could take photos on battlefields and in the towns and cities that were being shelled.

Two years after the war ended, in 1947, Edwin Robert Land demonstrated an amazing new device. His Polaroid Land camera could take and develop a positive print within sixty seconds. You didn't have to send the film to the darkroom because, in a very real way, the camera was the darkroom; it did the developing work all by itself. Land says he invented the camera because his daughter, then three years old, wondered if the pictures he took of her would be ready to see right away. Her question got him thinking about a way to make that happen.

The first Polaroid pictures were sepia, or shades of brown and cream. They had to be pulled out of the camera by hand and then "fixed" with a chemical stick. Placed on the market in 1948, the Polaroid sold for about $90 and weighed around four and a half pounds. Later improvements in the camera made the picture come out automatically. In time, the film was improved to be self-fixing and came in true black and white or color.

AMAZING FACTS

Film manufacturers were puzzled for years because batches of film that all contained the same kind of silver bromide crystals were wildly different in their sensitivity to light. It turned out that the gelatin that held the crystals was to blame. Gelatin comes from the hides of cattle; cattle that ate mustard plants made gelatin that created much more sensitive film than did gelatin from cattle with other diets. In 1926, scientists discovered that it was the mustard plant's sulfur-containing oil that made the difference. Manufacturers then went on to discover many other compounds that changed film's sensitivity and found ways to make these. They added them to the emulsion in carefully controlled amounts so that their film was sensitive to light the same way each time.

Ansel Adams (1902–1984)

Ansel Adams is known as the dean of modern photographers. He was a master of both the artistic and technical sides of photography and helped make it an accepted art form in his lifetime. Adams invented the zone system, which gives photographers a way to find the best exposure times for black and white photography. He fully describes this system in his book *The Negative and The Print*, which is still recommended reading for photographers. He worked with Edwin Land on the Polaroid Land process and wrote the *Polaroid Land Photography Manual*.

Adams took his first photograph with a Kodak Box Brownie camera on a family vacation to Yosemite National Park at about age fourteen, trying to capture the beauty of the mountains. However,

his pictures were so disappointing he decided to become a photofinishing apprentice so he could learn darkroom methods and start to make better photographs. He returned to Yosemite every summer and, in 1919, joined the Sierra Club, a conservation group dedicated to the Sierra Nevada wilderness. He became an expert mountaineer and conservationist. At the same time, he pursued a career in music, teaching himself to play the piano in hope of becoming a concert pianist. However, in about 1930 he realized that his "own personal satisfaction with the pictures was greater than with music."

Adams published many books of his photographs and methods. His subjects range from scenes of nature, for which he is best known, to portraits and photo-essays. He had already published two limited editions of his photographs when he met the photographer Paul Strand. Just looking at Strand's negatives inspired Adams to change from his soft-focus style to clear, crisp photography. In 1932, Adams and several other photographers formed Group f/64. The group only lasted two years, but it helped shape American photography by using crisp images instead of retouched, idealized pictures of the world. "A photograph is not an accident, it is a concept," Adams insisted.

A famous conservationist, Ansel Adams received the Sierra Club's Muir Medal (1963) and Presidential Medal of Freedom (1980). Asked why he took pictures of rocks when people were killing one another, he explained, "The understanding of the . . . world of nature will aid in holding the world of man together."

Ansel Adams at the Academy of Natural Sciences of Philadelphia in 1981. He was there to receive the Academy's Gold Medal for distinction in natural history art.

Photography in a New Light

The laser was invented in 1960. This device creates, amplifies (makes bigger), and then sends out a special kind of light called coherent light. This is made up of waves that are all the same wavelength and all in step with one another. Ordinary light is made up of many different wavelengths and phases. Laser light is very strong because, since all of its waves are the same frequency, or wavelength, they hit an object all at the same place and time. Lasers are used in many ways in industry and in medicine.

In the 1960s, laser research led to the development of the hologram. Holograms use laser light to make three-dimensional images. They record light wave patterns on a photographic plate or film. Holography is used with microscopy to study very small objects and large collections of atmospheric particles. As with photography in World War II, holography helps industry study stress and vibration in

Circular holograms in a Paris museum. Although they record laser light waves rather than visible light waves, a photographic plate or film is still used to record the image.

manufactured materials. Holograms have artistic uses as well. Some kinds of holograms are now placed on jewelry or on pictures that can be viewed from many angles. Many companies use holograms as emblems on credit cards.

Photography as Art

Since its first years, photography has served science and business, journalism and art. From the moment it was invented, art critics and photographers have debated whether photography was an art or a science. Edward Steichen and Alfred Stieglitz, both photographers in the first half of the twentieth century, worked for the recognition of photography as an art. By 1960, enough photographs had shown artistic value and had been used in artistic ways to end the argument. Galleries and museums showed photographs just as they did paintings. Photography, although used in science and journalism, was fully accepted as an art form.

Still, the lines between art and journalism are not clearly drawn. A good photographer, whether journalist or artist, must have an eye for composition and line and know how images can speak to the viewer. Mathew Brady, a photographer and historian, helped form our view of the Civil War with the thousands of

Mathew Brady photographed this wounded soldier in the Civil War. The many thousands of photos taken at that time are a valuable record of important events and everyday life.

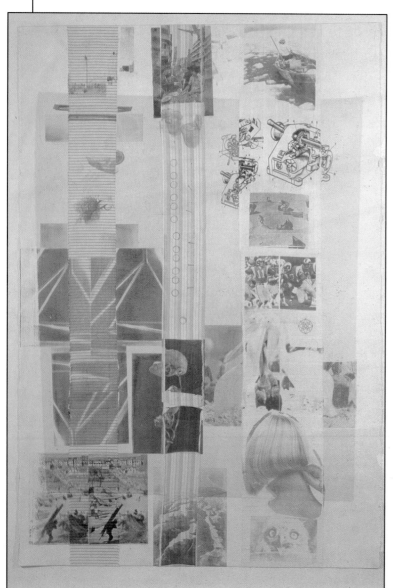

Robert Rauschenberg's Urban Ointment, *created in 1979, is a mixture of photographs and other images.*

photographs he took documenting battles and participants. Some of the best-known photojournalists include Alfred Eisenstaedt, who developed the technique of candid-camera news reporting and the picture story, Henri Cartier-Bresson, a French photographer famous for his portrayal of major political and social events, Margaret Bourke-White, who recorded many of the important events in the first half of the twentieth century, and David Seymour, a political photojournalist famous for his photos of children affected by World War II.

The best fashion photographers are artists with the camera. For example, Diane Arbus began in fashion but is best known for her striking photos of everyday and unusual people. Her work is like a mirror held up to American culture in the 1950s. In part, it shows the emptiness some people felt after the war, when many found that all the material things they had didn't make them truly happy.

Artists can make photographs speak about inner worlds as well as the world around us. Visual artists such as Andy Warhol, David Hockney, and Robert Rauschenberg brought their "painter's eye" and creative ideas to photography. They worked with the camera to make multiple images and patterns that were both clever and powerful. Since the sixties, these and other artists have creatively blended photography with other media, including computer imaging.

— Chapter 6 —
Cameras and Computers Unite

During the period that followed World War II, changes in electronics and computers made cameras better. For example, in the sixties and seventies, some camera viewfinders showed the photographer when a picture was in focus. Then cameras became even more automated. Technological improvements came not only from Europe and America, where the camera had been invented and improved, but from Japan.

As they did with cars, radios, and sound equipment, the Japanese took good ideas and made them better, developing cameras that offered new options at a good price. Japanese film became competitive with American film. In the 1960s, Japan joined America and Europe to became a world leader in camera technology; it has stayed competitive ever since.

Tiny Chips and Big Changes

When computer chips were put into cameras with telephoto lenses, many choices were suddenly available at the touch of a button. The camera could choose the right exposure and focus for portraits, close-up shots, panoramas, or pictures of sporting events that needed a fast exposure to capture motion. Cameras in the 1980s began to use electronic displays and sounds to tell the photographer dozens of pieces of information, including shutter speed, aperture, depth of field (which is how much of the area both in front of the subject and behind it will also be in focus when

AMAZING FACTS

Both special film and electronic sensors can record infrared light. Photographers can take infrared photos of cities at night that show traffic patterns and other features in terms of heat. Satellites are able to use sensors to scan infrared light reflected off the surface of planets and show how hot different features are. For example, since rivers are not as warm as plants, they reflect infrared light differently. Computers can take the numbers that measure these temperature differences and make false-color pictures and maps for scientists to study.

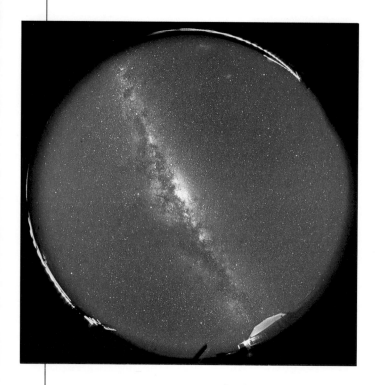

A view of the Milky Way taken by a special wide-angle camera that records the entire night sky from Las Campanas Observatory in Chile. Observatory buildings and lights can be seen around the edge of the image.

the subject is correctly focused), camera shake alert (which tells when the film will be exposed too slowly to be hand held), flash-charge completion to let you know when your flash is ready to go, and other options.

Some cameras can now be told to automatically "bracket" the exposure. Bracketing means that you take one picture a step faster and another a step slower than the light meter suggests. This helps get a good picture in difficult light conditions. In the nineties, some cameras have two or more focusing frames that blink to tell the photographer which parts of a scene are in focus and what the depth of field is for the picture about to be taken. Many cameras' flash attachments pop up automatically when the automatic light meter shows a flash is needed. In addition, film speed is read automatically now by most cameras so the photographer no longer has to set that information when changing from one film to another.

Since the camera has become so automated, many photographers want to have the choice of automatic or manual for certain pictures. So, for more money, many 35 mm cameras give both automatic and manual options on the same camera. The more expensive cameras also allow you to use many kinds of lenses and filters. With all these options, the cameras of today have become more automatic but also more complicated. A good computerized camera can do so many different things that it takes a while to learn to use it well.

New Answers to Old Problems

Since the 1940s, cameras could be preset and then give the photographer ten or fifteen seconds to run around in front of the camera and get in the picture. Now, a remote control unit can trigger the shutter so the photographer can snap the photo when standing in front of the camera or anywhere else.

Another photography problem that technology has solved is the old "red-eye" photo. When light from a flash reflects off the retina at the back of someone's eye through the wide-open iris, it causes spooky-looking red eyes in color pictures. This happens because the eye pupil hasn't had time to close down so the back of the eye, which is red, reflects the light back out again. Many modern cameras shoot out a beam of light just before the flash goes off so the irises in peoples' eyes automatically close enough to keep from looking red in the photo.

Another new kind of camera is really a remake of George Eastman's old idea. First available in the late 1800s, preloaded recyclable cameras returned in the 1990s, after a brief time in the 1980s when Kodak sold a throw-away camera that was both nonbiodegradable and nonrecyclable. In the 1880s version, the entire camera kept cycling back and forth between the customer and Kodak Company. In the 1990s version, in response to

A wide range of special effects filters is available to make even ordinary subjects exciting. In this photo, a diffractor filter has added colorful highlights to the sunlight reflecting from a rock pool.

environmental concerns, the company now recycles all the camera parts, including the camera case, battery, and film canister. The customer buys a new single-use camera when needed. Travelers find these very handy because they don't have to pack a camera. They give good (but not great) quality pictures at an affordable price, just as the first preloaded cameras did over a hundred years ago.

Films, Papers, and the Environment

Taken on fast film, the background to this photograph is blurred, emphasizing the speed of the motorcycle. This was achieved by tracking the bike in the camera viewfinder and pressing the shutter button at the same time. The technique is called "panning."

Film speeds for color prints are now available from 25, which is the slowest, to 3200, which is very fast. These speeds are rated by the International Standards Organization, or ISO, which assigns a speed number to each film so that photographers can set their exposures according to that information. Fast film allows for fast-action sports photos. Because it makes quick use of all available light, fast film is also good for low-light conditions. Slow films need more light, but they often give richer

detail. Some photographers like to carry more than one camera, loaded with different speeds of film, so they can switch from fast to slower speeds as needed.

Kodachrome, or K-14, is a high-quality slide film still used for book publishing and amateur use. However, it can only be developed at a few sites around the United States and the world because of the environmental dangers of its process. Unlike other films, K-14 does not actually have color in the film. The color is brought out in the high alkaline developer and high acidic bleach fixer. Since these chemicals are hard on the environment, governments try to limit how much they are used. However, all films use chemicals so they all stress the environment to some degree.

The Next Photo Revolution Has Arrived

Digital cameras get away from chemicals altogether because they record the photo on a computer chip instead of on film. Thus, digital cameras are more friendly to the environment than cameras that use film.

There are two main kinds of digital cameras. The one for everyday use is a CCD, a charge coupled device, that takes all the visual information at one time and stores it on a computer imaging chip (a chip that stores visual images) instead of film. It currently uses between four and seven megabytes of computer memory per image. The other kind of digital camera uses a linear array. This scans the image line by line. It gives better quality than the other digital system, but it takes much longer — about ten minutes instead of just a few seconds. The linear array system uses a huge amount of computer memory, about one hundred megabytes per image. Since it is about as slow as the daguerreotype with which photography began, it's not used to take pictures of live subjects since most people can't sit still that long. A much more expensive process, it's used mostly in high-quality publishing.

Pedro Meyer

Pedro Meyer's work often makes a political statement or shows something important about social issues. For example, one of his photos, called *English Tourist in Florida*, illustrates the issue of how his culture is always presented as exotic, while in reality, images of the exotic are to be found everywhere and in all peoples.

Pedro Meyer was born in Madrid, Spain, in 1935. He and his family moved to Mexico two years later, and he became a citizen of Mexico in 1942. A self-taught photographer, Meyer also curates, writes and lectures on photography, and is today one of the leading practitioners of digital image making in the world.

Meyer was the founding president of the Mexican Council of Photography, Mexico City, in 1977. He established and organized the first Colloquium of Latin American Photography, held in Mexico City in 1979, and two further colloquiums (conferences) held in Mexico City in 1981 and Havana, Cuba, in 1984.

Since the early 1980s, Meyer has become increasingly involved in the world of new technologies and their relationship to photography. In 1990, he produced the first photographic work with narration to be published on a CD-ROM, *I Photograph to Remember*, the story of the last years of his parents' lives. In 1993, "Truths and Fictions," a major exhibition of his digital photographic works produced over the last eight years, began an international tour. In 1994, an accompanying

A self portrait by Pedro Meyer.

CD-ROM of the same title was published in association with the exhibit. In 1995, *Truths and Fictions* was published as a book. Three other books on his work have been published to date: *Espejo de Espinas, Los Cohetes Duraron Todo el Dia*, and *Tiempos de America*.

He is the recipient of several photographic awards including the Bienal of Photography, Instituto Nacional de Bellas Artes, Mexico City, 1980 and 1983; Premio Internazionale di Cultura, City of Anghiari, Italy, 1984; Artist in residence Arizona Commission; and first prize of the Organización Internacional del Trabajao, OIT, in Santiago de Chile.

In 1987, Meyer received the John Simon Guggenheim Fellowship Grant, to photograph the United States. In 1992, he received a National Endowments of the Arts award in the U.S. as well as the U.S./Mexico Cultural Fund (Rockefeller) award to produce his one person exhibition "Truths and Fictions" under the auspices of the California Museum of Photography. This exhibition has toured throughout the Americas and Europe. His work is in private and public collections around the world.

Pedro Meyer's English Tourist in Florida.

Known for his documentary style, the respect he shows for his human subjects, and the strong statements his photos make about the world we live in, Meyer uses dense detail, intense light, and wide angles to give his photographs a special look. Though he has skill with the camera and the darkroom, now he only works in digital formats. He uses solely computers to create his work, and he continues to speak on social matters. Meyer cares about his culture and his work and is often asked to be a spokesperson for Latin American photographers.

Just because the weather is poor does not mean that you cannot take interesting photographs. A graduated mauve filter has added color to the sky of this misty landscape. Graduated filters are available in a wide range of colors, from subtle gray to fluorescent green.

Many photographers believe that digital cameras will replace film within the next ten years. They think that some artists may still use film, but the general public and print industry will probably use only digital photos.

Although they get away from the harsh chemicals of film, even digital cameras must still use paper to print a good photo. Now that whole forests of trees are used to make paper for the world, people are starting to think more carefully about how much paper they use. They often try to use recycled paper. But most photographs look clearest on new paper. The choice of paper a photographer uses in the dark-room can make a big difference in how a photograph looks. Some papers print pictures with higher contrast than others; some show up one kind of color more brightly than others. Paper choices, even for amateurs, include glossy or matte, Kodacolor or competing papers such as Ilford. Usually, better papers cost a little more but give better results.

Photography Can Be Simple

If you want to take pictures, but making your own darkroom seems like too much work and a digital camera is too expensive for you, don't worry. A lot can be learned just from practice with the simplest camera. Good pictures can be made with point-and-shoot cameras and film developed through the local store.

With all the lenses, filters, films, and papers available, it's easy to spend a fortune on camera equipment, and millions of people do just that. However, you can take high-quality pictures with a steady hand, a simple box camera, and some care for lighting and focus. Since expensive cameras are usually complicated to use, good advice for the new photographer is to start slowly and simply and build your equipment collection as you build your skills.

Photography's Gifts

The parent of movies and video, photography continues to be a powerful tool of communication, artistic expression, and science. As we've seen, photography began with the camera obscura, known about by scholars for thousands of years, which could project an image but not record it. Then, in a mere one hundred years, the daguerreotype and the calotype led to the wet plate and then the dry plate process, followed by roll film developed in a lab, and then Polaroid film developed in the camera itself.

Less than two hundred years after Niepce recorded the first photograph on a metal plate, we are now looking at photographs printed out from computers that scan images in filmless cameras capable of storing those images on microchips. Photography began as an invention just waiting to happen, but once invented, it not only changed with each new improvement, it changed the way people see their world and share it with one another.

> **AMAZING FACTS**
>
> Geologists use space photography to find faults that can show where earthquakes might occur. They also use it to study places that are hard to get to such as mountaintops and deserts.

A 15 mm fisheye lens has added drama to this photograph of a racing car. Because the lens makes everything appear small in the viewfinder, the photographer had to be extremely close to the action to fill the frame with the subject.

Timeline

1544 — Rainer Freisus builds a room-sized camera obscura to observe the solar eclipse of 1544 and then publishes a drawing of the device itself.

1550s — Gerolamo Cardano puts a glass lens on the hole of the camera obscura.

1685 — Johann Zahn puts a mirror in the box of the camera obscura to turn the image right side up before it hits the tracing paper on the glass.

1802 — Thomas Wedgwood and Sir Humphrey Davy use silver salts to create something they call a photogram, which they make by casting a shadow on a silver-salted surface.

1839 — Daguerreotype is presented to world as first photograph, invented by Joseph Nicéphore Niepce and Louis Jacques Mandé Daguerre. William Henry Fox Talbot and Sir John Herschel also create photographic processes.

1851 — Frederick Scott Archer develops the "wet plate" process.

1871 — Richard Leach Maddox develops dry plate photography — glass plates treated with a gelatine and silver-salt emulsion.

1888 — George Eastman develops roll film.

1889 — Eastman begins to market the Kodak camera loaded with this film.

1925 — The Leica, a thirty-five-millimeter camera, developed by Oskar Barnack of the Ernst Leitz company, is marketed for the first time.

1930 — Bela Gaspar invents Gasparcolor, which becomes, with improvements, Eastmancolor. Leopold Mannes and Leopold Godowsky develop the Kodachrome method of color slides.

1936 — The KineExacta camera is invented in Dresden, the first single-lens reflex camera.

1937 — Color slide film is put on the market.

1942 — Color negative film, which makes printed pictures, becomes available.

1947 — Polaroid Land camera is placed on the market.

1960s — The laser is invented, allowing development of hologram.

1980s — Computer chips are placed in cameras.

1990s — Digital cameras come on the market.

Further Reading

Ancona, George. *My Camera*. New York: Crown Publishers, 1992.

Chiaramonte, Giovanni. *The Story of Photography*. Translated by W. S. DiPiero. New York: Aperture, 1983.

Craven, John, and John Wasley. *Young Photographer*. New York: Sterling Publishing, 1981.

Fisher, Robert. *Trick Photography*. New York: M. Evans and Company, 1980.

Glassman, Carl. *Hocus Focus*. New York: Franklin Watts, 1976.

Jacobs, Jr., Lou. *You and Your Camera*. New York: Lothrop, Lee and Shepard, 1971.

Lauber, Patricia. *Seeing Earth from Space*. New York: Orchard Books, 1990.

Michell, Barbara. *Click! A Story about George Eastman*. Minneapolis, MN: Carolrhoda Books, 1986.

Palder, Edward L. *Magic with Photography*. New York: Grosset and Dunlap, 1969.

Weiss, Harvey. *Lens and Shutter*. Reading, MA: Young Scott Books, 1971.

Glossary

Aperture: The adjustable opening that lets light into a camera.

Bitumen of Judea: A brown or black flammable, tarlike substance used in lithography, a form of printing that relies on the fact that oil and water do not mix.

Digital camera: A camera with digital computer abilities. Digital computers record information by means of numbers. The digital camera does not need film but records onto computer memory.

Emulsion: A light-sensitive coating, usually of silver halide grains in a thin gelatin layer, on photographic film, paper, or glass.

Exposure time: Amount of time film is hit by light.

F-stop: A camera lens aperture setting that measures the focal length of any lens and helps decide how much light should be allowed to hit the film.

Filter: A glass disk screwed over the camera lens that screens out some light wavelengths while allowing other light wavelengths through to the camera.

Focal length: The distance between the lens and the place where it forms a sharp image on film or paper.

Focal point: A point where rays of light come together on a lens or mirror.

Infrared light: "Below red." Each color in the spectrum has its own wavelength, ranging from violet, which is the shortest wavelength seen by the human eye to red wavelengths, which are the longest. Infrared wavelengths are too long to be seen by the human eye.

Linear array: A way to scan an image line by line.

Matte: Flat, not shiny.

Megabytes: One million bytes. A byte is the amount of computer memory needed to store one character (a letter or a number) of a specific size.

Optics: The study of light perceived by vision, which is light with waves greater than X-rays and shorter than microwaves.

Telephoto lenses: Lenses that produce an enlarged image of a distant object.

Tones: Shades of a color, including shades of black and shades of white.

Index

Numbers in *italic* indicate pictures; numbers in **bold** indicate biographies